A Jog in Fog

by Jesse Griffin
illustrated by C. A. Nobens

Core Decodable 27

I0806527

McGraw Hill Education

Bothell, WA • Chicago, IL • Columbus, OH • New York, NY

MHEonline.com

Send all inquiries to:
McGraw-Hill Education
8787 Orion Place
Columbus, OH 43240-4027

ISBN: 978-0-02-135325-5
MHID: 0-02-135325-5

Printed in the United States of America.

7 8 9 LCR 25 24 23

Jack is a dog on a hilltop.

Jack cannot jog.
Jack cannot see in fog.

Jan is a frog at a pond.

Jan cannot jog in fog.

Jill is at the rocks.

Can Jill jog?

Jill can jog!

Jill can see in the fog!